EXPLORATION THROUGH THE AGES

THE VOYAGE OF MAGELLAN

Richard Humble

Illustrated by
Richard Hook

Franklin Watts
London · New York · Toronto · Sydney

© Franklin Watts 1988

First published in Great Britain in
1988 by
Franklin Watts
12A Golden Square
London W1

First published in the USA by
Franklin Watts Inc.
387 Park Avenue South
New York
N.Y. 10016

First published in Australia by
Franklin Watts Australia
14 Mars Road
Lane Cove
NSW 2066

UK edition ISBN: 0 86313 741 5
US edition ISBN: 0-531-10638-1
Library of Congress Catalog Card
No: 88-50376

Editor: Sue Unstead
Designer: Ben White
Picture research: Jan Croot
Maps: Hayward Art Group

Photographs:
Archivo General de Indias, Seville, 9
Museo de América, Madrid, 26
Museo Marítimo, Seville, 28
National Maritime Museum,
    Greenwich, 13

Printed in Belgium

JUN '90

Contents

The widening world

Five hundred years ago, mankind began an astonishing series of voyages of exploration, not to be equaled until our own century's voyages into space: the conquest of the oceans of the world.

These voyages happened at a time when knowledge of ships and the sea had advanced just far enough to enable men of vision and courage to achieve their goals. Like the first space flights, exploration of the seas was spurred on by competition between nations: the quickening race between the kingdoms of Portugal and Spain to become the richest trading nation in the world.

The prize in the race was rich indeed: the gold, silks, pearls and spices of the East Indies and China, or Cathay. The wealth and wonders of the Far East had been revealed to Europe by the earlier travels of Marco Polo and other explorers. But by 1450 the ancient overland route to Cathay had been blocked by hostile Arab traders. The race was now on to find a new route east – by sea.

Africa was the first land barrier to be passed by European seafarers. Portugal took the lead, probing farther and farther down the west coast of Africa. With each voyage, sailors brought back valuable experience in navigating by the unfamiliar stars, winds and currents south of the Equator.

In 1488 Bartolomeu Dias was the first European to round the Cape of Good Hope, opening the sea route from Europe to the Indian Ocean. Ten years later, Vasco da Gama reached India.

Spain replied by sending an Italian, Christopher Columbus, west across the Atlantic in search of a direct sea route to Cathay. Instead Columbus discovered the Caribbean, Central and South America (1492–1504). By 1515 Portugal's hold on the African sea route to the rich spice trade of the Indies appeared secure – unless Spain could discover an alternative westward route, somehow bypassing the land barrier of South America.

This was the challenge taken up by Ferdinand Magellan in 1519: the voyage destined to be the first to encircle the world.

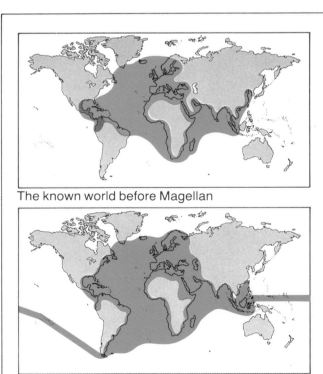

The known world before Magellan

The known world after Magellan

▷ *Top* This map shows the seas known to European sailors before Magellan's voyage, with South America still to be bypassed by sea.

Right Magellan's great discovery: not just the true size of the huge Pacific Ocean ("South Sea") but an open sea lane around the world.

△ The small, sturdy, three-masted ship called a *nao*: a type used by Portuguese and Spaniards alike on the great voyages of exploration. Its hold carried enough provisions for the crew to survive long ocean voyages (though in great hardship) and to ship home the rich cargoes of spices for which these costly, high-risk voyages were planned and made.

Dawn of adventure

The men who sailed on the great voyages of exploration did not embark in new ships that had been specially designed to survive the perils that lay ahead. The princes, merchants and bankers who put up the money for these expeditions cut every corner they could to save money. The ships of Magellan's day were ordinary merchant ships, usually old and often in need of extensive repairs.

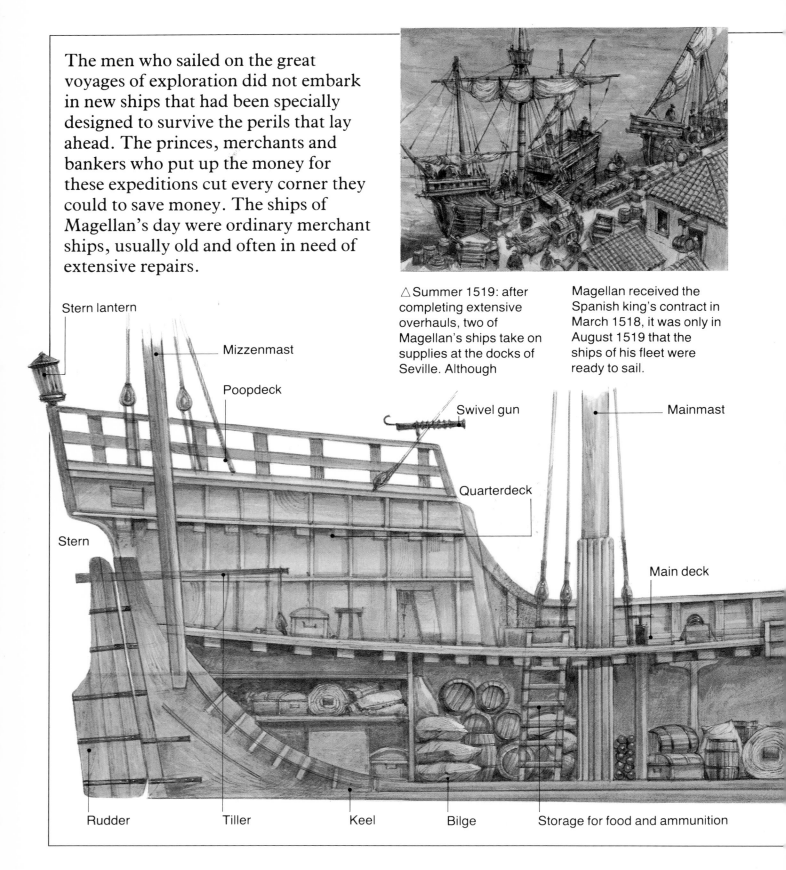

△ Summer 1519: after completing extensive overhauls, two of Magellan's ships take on supplies at the docks of Seville. Although

Magellan received the Spanish king's contract in March 1518, it was only in August 1519 that the ships of his fleet were ready to sail.

Stern lantern

Mizzenmast

Poopdeck

Swivel gun

Mainmast

Quarterdeck

Stern

Main deck

Rudder

Tiller

Keel

Bilge

Storage for food and ammunition

△ Seagull's eye view of the *Trinidad*'s crew setting sail: square sails on fore and mainmast, triangular lateen sail on the mizzenmast aft.

Such was the case with the five old *naos* provided for Magellan by King Charles I of Spain. They needed so many repairs and replacement timbers that it took Magellan 18 months to get them ready for his voyage to the Indies. His ship, the *Trinidad*, was probably no more than 27 m (90 ft) in length; the smallest, the *Santiago*, was about half the size. The crew on board varied from about 40 officers and men in the smallest ships to over 60 in the largest. The names of the ships were the *Trinidad* (Magellan's flagship), *San Antonio* (the largest), *Concepcion*, *Victoria* and *Santiago*.

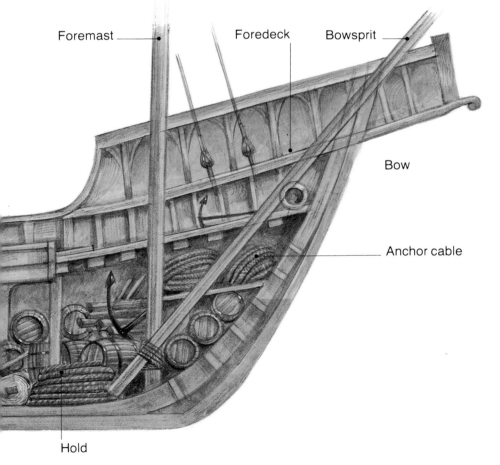

Foremast — Foredeck — Bowsprit

Bow

Anchor cable

Hold

◁ Probable interior layout of the *Trinidad*. Even in the biggest ships, conditions were cramped and spartan for both officers and men, and wet whenever the deck seams leaked in rough weather. All the ship's filth drained into the bilge, which had to be regularly cleaned out or "rummaged" on long voyages. For defense against pirates, the ships were armed with light swivel guns mounted on the rails. Magellan's *capitana* or flagship, the *Trinidad*, was the only ship in the fleet armed with cannon mounted on gun carriages: four in all.

Life on board

Every man aboard ship had his own special job. Navigation was shared by the captain and navigator. The master was responsible for the safe handling of the ship; the boatswain for the running of the crew. In addition to constant work on the rigging, the able seamen being the most experienced aloft, crewmen also worked under the direction of the ship's craftsmen. The ship's boy's special task was singing prayers at sunrise and sunset.

△ Even in the more sheltered accommodations aft, sleeping facilities were restricted, overcrowded, damp and increasingly dirty.

▽ The typical ship's company of Magellan's day was a team of tough professionals. Each had his own special job to do and sailed in hope of a share in the profits.

▽ The crews who sailed with Magellan included Spaniards, Portuguese, Germans, Italians, French, Flemings, Malays, Greeks and Africans.

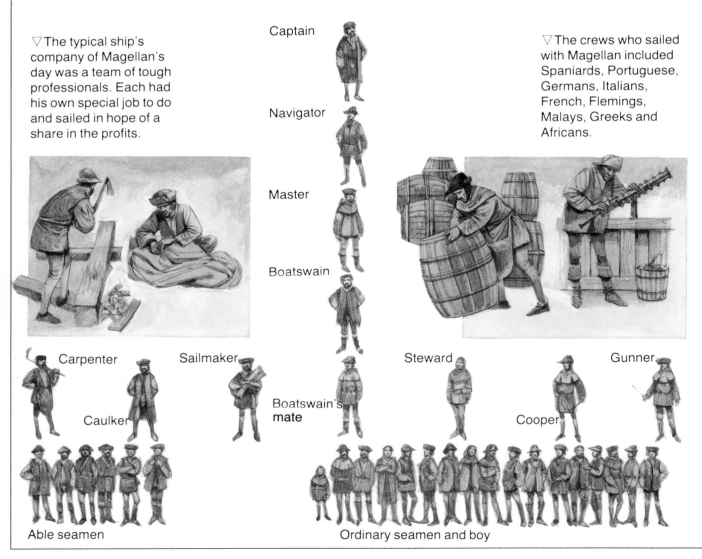

Captain

Navigator

Master

Boatswain

Carpenter

Caulker

Sailmaker

Boatswain's mate

Steward

Cooper

Gunner

Able seamen

Ordinary seamen and boy

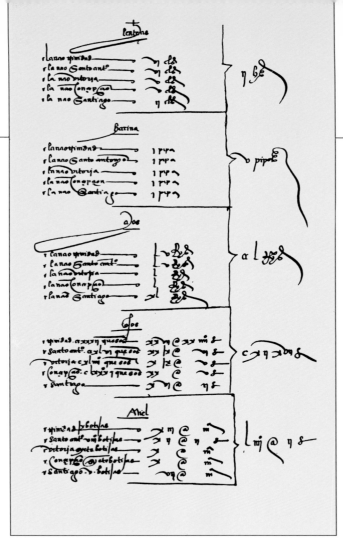

For long-distance ocean voyaging, outfitters chose food and drink that could be stored in barrels for the longest possible time. Drying and salting were the only methods of preserving meat, fish, fruit and vegetables. Although wine stood up better to storage in casks, water was vital for cooking as well as drinking – but water was the most difficult of all to keep fresh. The coopers, responsible for the condition of the casked food and water, had one of the most important jobs in the entire fleet. Constant inspections were needed to check on how the food and water stocks were surviving the voyage. The rule was that any cask of doubtful food or water had to be consumed at once.

△Cooking – nearly always by boiling – was done on deck, because of lack of space and the ever-present fear of fire. The cook's special iron stove was placed by the lee rail, where flames would blow away from the ship. A bucket of seawater was kept close by to douse any sparks.

▷Meals were served and eaten on deck, with sections of worn-out sailcloth spread out like tablecloths. As the voyage wore on, the stocks of iron-hard ship's biscuits became infested with weevils and worms which had to be patiently tapped out before eating.

Braving the wide oceans

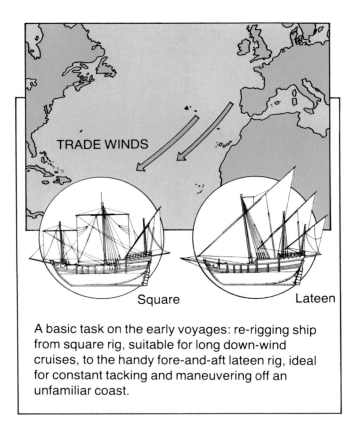

TRADE WINDS

Square   Lateen

A basic task on the early voyages: re-rigging ship from square rig, suitable for long down-wind cruises, to the handy fore-and-aft lateen rig, ideal for constant tacking and maneuvering off an unfamiliar coast.

The epic voyages of ocean exploration were far more perilous than the first manned flights to the Moon. The astronauts of the 1960s were able at all times to call for advice from their base, or even, in the event of dire emergency, to be brought home safely by remote control. But the men who sailed with Dias, Columbus, da Gama and Magellan sailed totally out of contact with their homelands for months, often taking years at a time, with death stalking them every mile of the way.

Once out at sea, the crews of the great ocean voyages of exploration were thrown completely on their own resources.

◁Pitching to the high Atlantic swell, the ships of Magellan's fleet set out on the opening leg of the voyage: the long south-westerly run to make landfall on the South American coast. When

Magellan sailed from Spain in fall 1519, men embarking on a long-distance voyage could count on at least two months' sailing in relatively familiar seas, winds and currents.

They had to be able to repair and re-rig their ships if damaged or dismasted by bad weather. If necessary – as happened on the fourth voyage of Columbus in 1504 – they had to be able to abandon their original ships, strip them of all useful material, and build new vessels from local materials and timbers salvaged from the wrecks. There was no other way of getting home, no friendly ships to pick them up, and no relief expeditions to come to their aid. If stranded on an unknown shore, survivors knew that they might have to live out the rest of their lives without ever seeing another ship from their homes.

They faced death from storm and shipwreck, and death from hunger and thirst. The longer the voyage, the surer was the likelihood of death by disease – not just scurvy from the lack of fresh fruit and vegetables, but typhoid from foul and putrid drinking water. They also risked food poisoning from rotted provisions, "rat-bite fever" from the squeaking prey that hunted desperately for food in the stinking holds, and typhus from lice swarming on dirty bodies and clothing. First aid was rough and ready. Perhaps it was just as well that these ships carried no doctors, for European medicine of the early 1500s probably killed as often as it cured.

To face and survive such hardships and dangers, men needed much more than mere physical toughness. As with sailors in all ages, they learned to rely not only on each other but on their leaders' ability to penetrate the unknown and bring them safely home.

The navigator's art

By the time Magellan's fleet sailed from Spain, European sailors had been using the compass, the basic tool of navigation, for nearly 400 years. But this could only indicate the ship's direction. It was the task of the navigator to calculate the ship's position from day to day.

For such a calculation, the navigator had to know how far north or south of the Equator his ship was – the latitude – and how far east or west – the longitude – from its last known position.

By the early 1500s, navigators had all the equipment they needed to calculate latitude with reasonable accuracy. Using quadrant, cross-staff or astrolabe, they measured the height or altitude of the Sun or of prominent stars above the horizon.

They then checked tables listing known altitudes to read off the correct latitude for the appropriate date.

The problem was longitude, calculated by the passage of time from the ship's point of departure. In Magellan's day, it was determined by the calendar and by constantly turned hourglasses. More than 250 years were to pass before accurate timekeepers, or chronometers, enabled navigators to determine longitude precisely.

◁The all-important noon sight, with the Sun at its highest point in the sky. The navigator aligns the central cross-piece of the astrolabe with the horizon, and peers through the holes in the swivelling pointer to aim at the Sun. An assistant stands by to check the altitude tables.

▽The basic tools of navigation in the 16th century: compass (*right*) and astrolabe. The brass box contains a piece of lodestone. This naturally magnetic iron ore was used to restore magnetism to the soft iron compass needle.

Under strange stars

As the ships pushed farther and farther south from the familiar waters of Europe and North Africa, one of the most awe-inspiring experiences was the change in the night sky.

The Pole Star, the central point of the heavens in the Northern Hemisphere, dropped closer to the northern horizon every night. At last it vanished altogether, followed by the familiar sickle of the Great Bear as well.

And in their place, rising majestically above the southern horizon, there rose the beautiful new constellation of the Southern Cross.

The Portuguese were the first Europeans to experience this phenomenon in the 1450s and 1460s on their coast-hugging voyages around the West African "bulge" and onward across the Equator. By Magellan's day, some 70 years later, it was a familiar natural occurrence on all voyages to southern latitudes. And the navigators were already at work, plotting the movements of the southern stars for the benefit of those who would follow.

▽ Night in the South Atlantic. The men of Magellan's fleet, steering by the stern lantern of the flagship, find time to mutter a quick prayer as the Southern Cross rises above the horizon.

Yet although there were plenty of experienced sailors to reassure the "first-time" members of Magellan's expedition, nothing could dispel the sense of wonder at this change in the heavens felt by those who had never seen it before. One such was Antonio Pigafetta, who described the Southern Cross as "a cross with five extremely bright stars straight toward the west, those stars being exactly placed with regard to each other". He also noted that "The Antarctic Pole is not so starry as the Arctic. Many small stars clustered together are seen, which have the appearance of two clouds of mist." To this day, these are known to astronomers as the Magellanic Clouds.

A more practical source of comfort was that the compass continued to point steadily to the north. Yet to these Catholic sailors, the nightly presence of the great cross in the sky must have suggested divine protection.

Gateway to the South Sea

From his earlier voyages around Africa, Magellan knew that south of the Equator the seasons are reversed, with winter in the north being summer in the south.

After reaching the Brazilian coast in December 1519, Magellan planned to follow the South American coast at least as far as 45°S: halfway between the Equator and the South Pole. There he would seek out a suitable anchorage where he could overhaul the ships, replenish food and water supplies, and allow the men to rest through the winter of the Southern Hemisphere before resuming the voyage.

On March 31, 1520 Magellan found the winter anchorage he wanted at San Julian, on the coast of modern Argentina. By now the voyage had already lasted six times longer than the first Atlantic crossing by Columbus, and there was no sign of a westward route past this desolate, apparently unending continent. Though Magellan's crew was willing to carry on, his Spanish officers were not.

Within 48 hours of arriving at San Julian, the officers of the *San Antonio*, the *Victoria*, and the *Concepcion* had declared a mutiny. Without the loyalty of the seamen, who refused to follow the rebel

officers, Magellan would never have been able to recover the three ships and crush the mutiny.

A month later, to keep up morale, Magellan sent the *Santiago* scouting southward down the coast, but on May 22, 1520 she was wrecked 70 miles south of San Julian. Only one man was drowned in the wreck, and the 37 survivors

▷Leaving the shattered wreck of the *Santiago* astern, Magellan's ships reduce sail to storm canvas as they begin the passage of the gale-lashed strait. They had to struggle against appalling weather all the way, in water so deep that it was impossible to cast anchor. The only way to secure the ships was by lines to the shore. Much time was wasted by the loss of contact with the deserting *San Antonio*. Magellan sent the *Victoria* all the way back to the Atlantic entrance of the strait in a vain search for the missing ship before giving the order to press on to the west.

managed to struggle back to San Julian in an exhausting overland march. But Magellan decided to take no further risks. It was not until October 18, 1520 that the fleet headed south again.

Three days later, Magellan found the eastern entrance to the strait which he had always sworn existed: a narrow inlet, lashed by screaming gales and flanked by sheer, snow-capped mountains. It took the ships over a month to negotiate the strait, during which time the *San Antonio* deserted and headed home to Spain. But on November 28 the *Trinidad*, *Concepcion* and *Victoria* finally emerged from the maze of islands at the western end of the strait and headed out into the "South Sea."

Agony in the Pacific

The scene was one of misery aboard the *Trinidad* and her two sister ships during the terrible first crossing of the Pacific Ocean, for the crews were ravaged by scurvy, starvation and thirst. "We were three months and twenty days without getting any kind of fresh food," wrote a survivor. "We ate biscuit which was no longer biscuit, but a powder of biscuit swarming with worms, for they had eaten the good. It stank strongly of the urine of rats. We drank yellow water that had been putrid for many days."

So weakened were the men that they could never have survived a storm, and Magellan thankfully named this tranquil new ocean "Pacific." "Had not God given us so good weather we would all have died of hunger in that exceeding vast sea. In truth I believe no such voyage will ever be made again." At last, after recrossing the Equator and heading west in a desperate attempt to reach Japan, they sighted green and fertile islands – the Marianas – on March 6, 1521.

▷ On entering the Pacific, Magellan headed for the Moluccas, which he knew lay 4° S of the Equator. But European mapmakers had greatly underestimated the true circumference of the Earth. Magellan found only empty sea at 4° S: the Moluccas lay nearly 7,000 miles to the west. Total disaster was only averted by his decision to try for a landfall in Japan by running west along Latitude 12° N, which brought him to the Marianas instead.

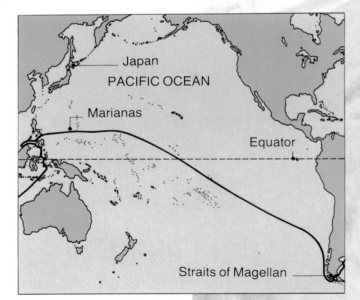

Landfall in the Philippines

Sick, starving, and desperately weak though they were, Magellan's men got no rest in the Marianas. The islanders turned out to be tireless thieves, swarming out to the ships in their outrigger canoes and stealing everything not nailed down. When they stole the longboat towed astern by the *Trinidad*, Magellan had to rouse his weary men to action. It was vital to get the longboat back; boats were essential for exploring unknown coasts where the bigger ships dared not venture too close inshore.

Magellan toured the ships, picking 40 of the fittest men, and led them ashore to punish the islanders and retrieve the longboat. Before they burned the native huts, the Europeans snatched up all the food they could carry: coconuts, fruit, sweet potatoes and fish. This plundered stock of food gave Magellan's crews just enough strength to raise anchor and push on to the west in search of a more friendly resting-place.

Their next landfall was the eastern Philippine Islands, sighted on March 16, a week after leaving the Marianas. This time Magellan took no chances. He sought out an uninhabited island, Homonhon, on which his men could rest and recover their strength. The Philippine islanders soon made contact and gave the ships a friendly welcome,

▽ From seemingly certain death in mid-ocean to an abundance of plenty: Magellan's starving crewmen gather food on the island of Homonhon.

willingly trading food for trinkets such as red caps, mirrors, combs and bells.

After an eight-day rest, Magellan moved on to the west. On March 28 the ships arrived off Limasawa, where Magellan's gifts were well received by the local chief, Rajah Calambu. Communication proved easy because Magellan's Malay slave could understand the islanders' Tagalog language. Rajah Calambu offered to guide Magellan's ships to the island of Cebu, where they would find ample supplies of food with which to continue their voyage to the Spice Islands.

The ships reached Cebu on April 7, where the ruler, Rajah Humabon, was impressed by Magellan's firm but tactful bearing, his fair dealing, and the obvious power of the weapons which his men demonstrated to the Cebu islanders. Humabon even agreed that he and his people would become Christians.

But this promising start ended in disaster on April 27, 1521. Magellan rashly agreed to attack the defiant ruler of nearby Mactan Island, but his tiny force of less than 50 men was driven back by overwhelming numbers, and Magellan was killed in the retreat to the ships.

◁ Thanks to his diplomacy and fair dealing, Magellan not only won the respect of the islands' ruling chiefs, but persuaded them to accept Christianity. Here he presents a statue of the Christ Child and other gifts for Rajah Humabon of Cebu.

△ A crossbowman gives a demonstration to curious islanders. Magellan tried not to rely on displays of European firepower to impress the Filipinos. But his attempt to demonstrate it in battle on the island of Mactan turned out to be a fatal mistake.

The Spice Islands at last

▽ While the coopers seal the casks of precious cloves, the *Victoria* is careened (leaned over) on the beach and her leaks are plugged. Seaweed and barnacles, which would otherwise slow the ship under sail, were burned off: a technique known as "breaming." Such regular maintenance was needed at least once a year.

Magellan's death shattered the myth that the Spaniards were invincible, and Rajah Humabon of Cebu turned against them. Deprived of Magellan's leadership and now under divided command, the three ships set off on an aimless voyage through the islands of the southern Philippines – though the Moluccas actually lay less than three weeks' sailing from Cebu.

This stage of the voyage lasted about six months, during which time manpower became a serious problem. The hardships and casualties of the voyage had reduced the total strength of the fleet by nearly half – to about 130 – not enough to man all three ships safely. On the advice of fleet pilot Joao Carvalho, the *Concepcion* was stripped of all useful cargo and gear and abandoned, her crew being shared between the *Trinidad* and the *Victoria*. At last, under Carvalho's faltering direction, they sighted the Moluccas, or Spice Islands, on November 6, 1521 – more than two years after leaving Spain.

The Sultan of Tidore in the Moluccas was delighted to welcome the Spaniards,

22

as the Portuguese had supported his rival, the Sultan of Ternate. He gladly agreed to trade with the Spaniards, and both the *Trinidad* and the *Victoria* took on rich cargoes of cloves and other spices highly prized in European markets.

There was no time to lose, as the seasonal easterly winds of the Indies had begun, vital for a fast passage southwest to the Cape of Good Hope. But on the eve of departure, the *Trinidad* sprang a serious leak. It was decided that the *Victoria* should sail at once for the Cape.

△ Careening also offered the chance to replace rotted planking and structural timbers. A carpenter is seen at work on the shaping of a new frame. When a ship had to be abandoned, its soundest timbers were often re-used.

When she was repaired and fit for sea again, the *Trinidad* would attempt to recross the Pacific and return to Spain via the Magellan Strait. Under the command of Juan Sebastian del Cano, crewed by 47 men with 13 Moluccans who had agreed to journey to Spain, the *Victoria* weighed anchor on December 21, 1521.

23

Homeward bound

The *Victoria's* lone voyage home to Spain was as desperate an ordeal as the first crossing of the Pacific. This time the route and course were well enough known in advance. But as the *Victoria* was a Spanish ship in jealously guarded Portuguese waters, the need to keep well clear of prowling Portuguese warships added thousands of miles to her homeward voyage.

Del Cano left Indonesia at the island of Timor on January 25, 1522. He then headed more than 3,500 miles southwest across the southern Indian Ocean, steering well below the latitude of the Cape of Good Hope. On this long haul all the fresh food taken aboard in the Moluccas had been eaten by the time the *Victoria* turned west toward the Cape on March 22. Her crew had to battle the cold winds and mighty seas of the "Roaring Forties" on a starvation diet of rice.

The *Victoria* finally rounded the Cape into the South Atlantic on May 19 with her foremast and yard split by a storm, slowing her even more. As she limped northward in the Atlantic, 21 men died of hunger and scurvy. Once again, the survivors were facing a desperate race against time.

◁Ordeal in the "Roaring Forties," the gale-lashed seas between Latitudes 40° and 50°S. The weakened canvas of the foresail is ripped and torn as the *Victoria*'s exhausted crew tries to keep her under way. In such seas there was a constant danger of the ship being "pooped" – taking a breaking wave over its stern and capsizing. Lashed to the mainmast to give him a secure footing, del Cano struggles to take a noon sight that will confirm the ship's latitude. Any serious navigation error could mean a landfall on the African coast, and arrest by the Portuguese.

The survivors return

By the middle of July 1522, del Cano was left with fewer than 30 men fit enough to lay hand to a rope. He had no choice but to steer for the Portuguese Cape Verde Islands, west of the African "bulge." Without food, he knew, all the *Victoria*'s dying crew were doomed.

At the Cape Verdes, del Cano tried to convince the Portuguese that the *Victoria* had sailed from Spanish America, and had been driven off course by a storm. The bluff nearly worked, but the *Victoria*'s landing party had only sent off two boatloads of rice when one of her men was caught with a packet of cloves. The secret was out: the *Victoria* could only have come from the Portuguese Indies. All 13 men of the shore party were thrown in jail while del Cano hastily headed back out to sea.

At last, on September 6, 1522, almost three years to the day, the *Victoria* entered the bay of San Lucar at the mouth of the Guadalquivir, sailing up river to anchor off Seville two days later. Only 18 men, most of them sick, had survived the ordeal of the voyage. One of them was the Italian Antonio Pigafetta, who proudly recorded that "we had sailed 14,460 leagues [43,380 miles] and completed the circuit of the world."

The *Trinidad* was not so lucky, being captured in the Moluccas by the Portuguese. Only four of her crew of 54 survived, eventually returning to Spain in 1525.

▽ The bustling riverfront and port of Seville, painted 50 years after Magellan's fleet sailed. In the middle looms the Cathedral. There, on September 8, 1522, del Cano led all the survivors of the *Victoria* who could walk to give thanks for their salvation. On the far bank, ships load and unload cargo; others are seen on the near bank being careened and overhauled before setting out on their next ocean voyage.

△ The *Victoria*'s precious
26 tons of spices are
weighed for pricing. They
were sold for 10,000
times their cost of
purchase – enough to pay
for the entire expedition;
but they made only a
small profit on the costs.

▷ Staggering through the
streets to give thanks at
Seville's Cathedral, each
man carrying a lighted
candle, the *Victoria*'s
surviving crewmen horrify
the well-fed citizens of
Seville with their gaunt
and tormented
appearance. Del Cano
later received a coat of
arms and a small
pension, but because the
profits of the voyage were
so small, none of the men
was ever paid in full for
his service.

Legacy of riches

So ended the most incredible sea voyage of the age of exploration, with 18 out of 250 men coming home. Magellan and del Cano had discovered the sea route around the world – a discovery hailed by the Spanish historian Gonzalo Fernandez de Oviedo. "The track the *Victoria* followed is the most wonderful thing and the greatest novelty that has ever been seen from the time God created the first man and ordered the world unto our own day." No human voyage of such importance would be made until Apollo 11 landed on the Moon 447 years later.

Wonderful though it was, the first voyage around the world failed to win immediate wealth and profit for Spain.

▽ The face of Ferdinand Magellan. The Latin inscription on top describes him as "The Most Famous Conqueror of the Antarctic Strait" – still known as the Strait of Magellan.

▷ Sixty years after the *Victoria*'s return to Seville, one of Spain's rich "Manila galleons" takes on cargo for the eastward crossing of the Pacific Ocean from the Philippines to Panama.

The discovery of the huge Pacific Ocean dashed the hopes of opening up an easy westward sea route to the Indies by following the track which Magellan had sailed. The ships of the day were too small and too slow to cover such vast distances on regular trading voyages. Spain did return to exploring the Pacific in the 1570s, but with ships sailing from Panama – not direct from Spain.

But these later voyages could not have been made without the knowledge that del Cano had brought home. The Philippine Islands, Magellan's last great discovery before his death, became Spain's most important colony in the Pacific and remained so for nearly 350 years.

With the Spanish Philippines receiving all the rich trade goods of the Far East, Magellan's dream was eventually realized by the Spanish galleons. These big, fast, well-armed ships carried goods eastward across the Pacific Ocean from the Philippines to Panama, where they were transported overland before crossing the Atlantic to Spain. Though Magellan and most of his sailors never lived to see it, this was their true memorial.

△ The real reason why the great voyages of exploration were made: luxury goods and trading profits for wealthy Europeans. Within 100 years of Magellan's death, the trail blazed by the ocean pioneers of Portugal and Spain was being eagerly followed by the East India Companies of England, the Dutch Republic and France. The "age of empire" had begun.

Glossary

Aft Towards the stern of a ship.

Astrolabe Navigator's instrument for measuring the altitude, or height, of the Sun and stars, to calculate the ship's latitude.

Bilge The lowermost "floor" of a ship, on either side of the keel, where the ship's internal water collects.

Boatswain The warrant officer in charge of sails, rigging, anchors, cables, and all day-to-day work aboard ship.

Breaming Lighting fires to burn off weeds and barnacles from the underside of a beached ship.

Careen To heel over the hull of a beached ship for cleaning or repairs.

Caulking Hammering waterproof material, or pouring hot pitch, between planks to prevent leaking.

Cooper Ship's craftsman responsible for making and repairing wooden barrels.

Cross-staff Early instrument used by navigators to measure the height of the Sun or stars.

Demarcation, Line of Imaginary line drawn north and south down the Atlantic Ocean by decree of Pope Alexander VI (1494). Lands to the east of the line were granted to Portugal, lands to the west of the line to Spain.

Draught The depth of water a ship draws, especially when loaded.

Fore Towards the bow, or front, of a ship.

Lateen Triangular fore-and-aft sail.

Latitude Distance measured in degrees north or south of the Equator.

▽ The track of the *Victoria*, 1519-22. The next such voyage, by Francis Drake in 1577-80, would discover an alternative route from Atlantic to Pacific: bypassing Cape Horn on the open sea, south of the Magellan Strait.

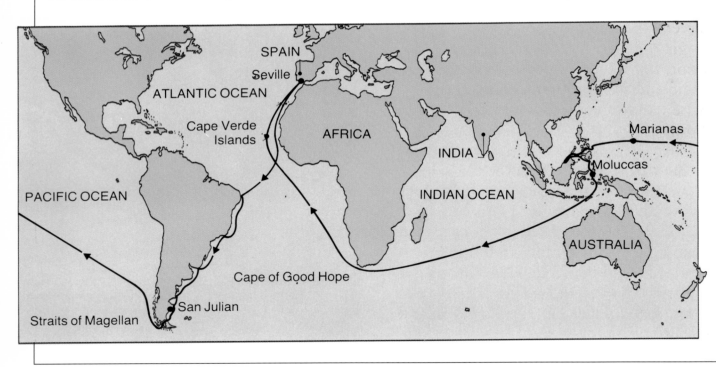

Timechart

Lee The downwind side of a ship, which does not have the wind blowing on it (from the Dutch *lij*, meaning shelter).
Longitude Distance measured east or west of an imaginary line connecting both Poles of the Earth.
Meridian A line of longitude.
Mizzen The third or aftermost mast of a ship.
Nao Three-masted ship built for carrying cargo, used in early voyages of exploration by both Portugal and Spain.
Quadrant A quarter-circle of wood or brass, the earliest navigator's instrument for measuring height of Sun or stars.
Quarterdeck The upper deck at the stern of a ship, aft of the mainmast, from which the ship was commanded.
Reaching Sailing at right-angles to the direction of the wind.
Reefing Reducing the area of a sail to prevent damage in high winds.
Rigging All ropes and cables used for supporting a ship's masts and spars, and for hoisting, lowering or trimming sails to the wind.
Running Sailing downwind, using the wind's full strength.
Tacking Changing direction of a ship by steering a zig-zag course to make headway against the wind.
Watch Division of the ship's crew, usually into port (lefthand side) and starboard (righthand side) This enables the men to serve alternating 4-hour periods of duty (also known as watches), resting when off watch.

1295 Marco Polo returns to Venice from his overland journey to Cathay (China).
1419 Portugal discovers the Madeira Islands.
1445 Portugal discovers the mouth of the Senegal River in West Africa.
c. 1480 Ferdinand Magellan born in northern Portugal.
1488 Bartolomeu Dias of Portugal rounds the Cape of Good Hope, reaching the Indian Ocean.
1492 Christopher Columbus, crossing the Atlantic Ocean, discovers the West Indies for Spain.
1498 Vasco de Gama of Portugal reaches Calicut in India.
1500 Pedro Cabral of Portugal lands on the coast of Brazil.
1513 Vasco Nunez de Balboa discovers the "South Sea" (the Pacific Ocean) west of the Panama Isthmus and claims all lands bordering it for Spain.
1517 Ferdinand Magellan leaves Portugal to seek service in Spain.
1519 Magellan sails from Spain with five ships to find a southern entrance to the "South Sea."
1520–21 Magellan crosses the Pacific Ocean and reaches the Philippine Islands, where he is killed in battle.
1521–22 Sebastian del Cano, one of Magellan's navigators, completes the first voyage around the world in the *Victoria*.

Index

PRINTED IN BELGIUM BY
proost
INTERNATIONAL BOOK PRODUCTION

Detroit City Ordinance 29-85, Section
29-2-2(b) provides: "Any person who
retains any library material or any part
thereof for more than fifty (50) calendar days beyond the due date shall be
guilty of a misdemeanor."

The number of books that may be
drawn at one time by the card holder is
governed by the reasonable needs of the
reader and the material on hand.

Books for junior readers are subject
to special rules.

JUN   '90